It's Not My Fault

150 Hilarious Excuses Every Tennis Player Should Know

JOSHUA SHIFRIN

FOREWORD BY PETER BODO

Skyhorse Publishing

Skyhorse Publishing books may be purchased in bulk at special discounts for
sales promotion, corporate gifts, fund-raising, or educational purposes. Special
editions can also be created to specifications. For details, contact the Special Sales
Department, Skyhorse Publishing, 307 West 36th Street, 11th Floor, New York,
NY 10018 or info@skyhorsepublishing.com.

Skyhorse® and Skyhorse Publishing® are registered trademarks of Skyhorse
Publishing, Inc.®, a Delaware corporation.

Visit our website at www.skyhorsepublishing.com.

10 9 8 7

Library of Congress Cataloging-in-Publication Data is available on file.

Interior images by Ian Baker. Tennis ball images by iStock.

Cover design by Tom Lau
Cover illustration credit: Ian Baker

ISBN: 978-1-5107-3053-3
Ebook ISBN: 978-1-5107-3054-0

Printed in China

To my tennis-loving son,
Gilad, and my sports-crazy son,
Idan—you are my everything!

Table of Contents

Acknowledgments

Like any worthwhile endeavor, success is rarely achieved alone. And the completion of *It's Not My Fault* was clearly not an individual accomplishment. I would like to take this opportunity to thank several instrumental players that had key roles in helping me with this project.

First and foremost, I want to thank my father, David Shifrin. He helped me in countless ways, and I can honestly say that this book would not have been completed without his immense assistance. Thanks, Dad!

As always, I need to thank my wife, Maya, and my boys, Gilad and Idan, for putting up with my highs and lows while I wrote this book.

I would like to thank my good friend Adam Broder for his tremendous support of my writing.

And last, I want to thank my editor, Julie Ganz, who was right there with me every step of the way.

Thank you to everyone who helped me along this journey.

Foreword

*T*ennis is a game chock full of traditions. You raise your hand in good-natured apology after winning a point with the aid of the net cord. No matter how bitter a defeat, you trudge to the net after the match ends and shake hands. If your opponent calls a ball "out" and you feel it was good, you can ask, "Are you sure?" but that's it. You don't argue, insist, or take a swing at the guy.

The traditions extend to spectators at tournaments, too. You don't cheer a player's errors. You only move about the arena during odd-game changeovers. You refrain from crying "out" or otherwise disrupting a point while the ball is in play.

You know the refrain, "Silence, please."

At Wimbledon, you must wear predominantly white if you have aspirations to set foot on a court. At the US Open, you do the Funky Chicken dance if the camera happens to light on you during a changeover and projects your image on the Jumbotron. If you're local at the Australian Open and someone yells out, "Aussie, Aussie, Aussie," you are morally obliged to shout back, "Oi, oi, oi."

Traditions, traditions, traditions.

Some of these habits and behaviors are held more dear than others, but none has the sheer universality and popularity of simple excuse making. Tennis players, it seems, have an excuse ready for any loss, whether it's personal or one suffered by a hero.

I lost to my cousin Herman yesterday because they put too much caramel in the part-skim no-foam double-shot caramel macchiato I had shortly before we played. Rafael Nadal lost to Roger Federer because a ballboy gave Rafa the wrong ball to serve at a critical break point.

Excuses.

Josh Shifrin has examined them, collected them, pondered them, and undoubtedly used them, liberally and shamelessly, in his woebegone career as a tennis hacker. That's what makes this little book so valuable, such a worthy addition to the tennis bookshelf in your home or local library. Think of *It's Not My Fault* as a tennis player's version of *The Joy of Cooking*; it's indispensable, at least if you hope to continue skating through life imagining that you can actually play this game.

In addition to compiling a vast rogue's gallery of shameless, pathetic excuses for poor tennis play (along with some very reasonable ones), Shifrin has also unearthed some marvelous, delusional, or simply weird statistics and anecdotes involving the top pro players.

For example, when contemplating the delicious excuse "I was just too inconsistent," Shifrin reminds us that this excuse won't always fly. At least it didn't for Grand Slam champion Yevgeny Kafelnikov. The Russian former star holds the record for the most unforced errors at a Grand Slam singles match with the 112 he accumulated during his 2000 French Open clash with Fernando Vicente. The fly in the ointment: Kafelnikov never got to employ the excuse because . . . he won the match.

Some people, Shifrin writes, will try to blame a loss on the fact that there were actually people watching the match. And Lord knows, that can be nerve-racking. So how do you explain the fact that Li Na defeated Francesca Schiavone to win the 2011 French Open final with 116 million of Li's fellow Chinese looking on—and a global audience later estimated at 330 million viewers?

Breaking a string during a match and having to default because you don't have a backup racket is a boneheaded move, especially if it happens early in your $60 per hour, prime-time hour at the indoor courts. Now imagine how stupid Goran Ivanisevic felt when he was defaulted from a match in the 2000 Samsung Open when he ran out of strung rackets during his match with Hjung-Taik Lee. Ivanisevic was defaulted for not having appropriate equipment.

There you have it. I don't know about you, but I've always enjoyed books that deal in the trivia and minutiae of the game. Sometimes, you just don't feel up to reading verbose, colorful paeans to the gods of tennis and their dramatic exploits. Sometimes, a little lighter fare is in order. Sometimes, it's good to just come across a little-known fact, or to recognize yourself in a thumbnail sketch, and sit back and laugh.

This book is there for you at those times.

—Peter Bodo, October 2017

Introduction

I love tennis! I love everything about the sport. From watching the pros play at the highest level, to reading books and articles, to discussing the game with my friends. But like most of us, I would have to say that my favorite part of tennis is grabbing my racket, lacing up my sneakers, and actually hitting that little, yellow, fuzzy ball back and forth across the net.

It's all just so exhilarating. The physical exertion. The mental focus. And at the end of the match, is there anything better than walking away victorious?! Basking in the thrill of victory after a hard-fought match is simply a high like no other.

But wait just a gosh darn minute! What about the other side of the coin? I can't even bear to say it . . . let alone think it. Dare you say, What happens when one loses a match? That lowest of lows. What has aptly been called the "Agony of Defeat."

Well, for all of you weekend warriors who have surely tasted that most bitter of pills, there is finally a solution to your misery. For in *It's Not My Fault*, I am here to let you know that a painful loss is made much more tolerable with the simple knowledge that . . . as the late Robin Williams so sensitively told Matt Damon in *Good Will Hunting*, "It's not your fault."

Surely losing in tennis couldn't be due to the fact that your backhand is lousy. Or because you double-faulted over and over again. And of course the fact that you're thirty pounds overweight couldn't possibly be the reason why your opponent used you to dust up the court. **Impossible!!!**

So how can we make sense of this most improbable of outcomes? How does the world continue to rotate in a universe where you have lost to a clearly inferior opponent? Well, fret no longer, because in *It's Not My Fault*, we've got the answer.

So unburden yourself from the questions, "How could this have happened? How could I be such a failure? How could I (gulp) be a loser?" Because if you can't figure out why you just lost, you'll likely find the reason in *It's Not My Fault: 150 Hilarious Excuses Every Tennis Player Should Know*!

Top Ten Professional Excuses

My parents always told me that if you want to be the best, you have to learn from the best. And in my opinion, if you truly want to come up with the best tennis excuses, you need to look to the pros for guidance. So without further ado, here are the top ten excuses ever uttered by a tennis professional!

Number 10:

"I have to be honest. I think I lost because I wasn't wearing a bra."—Pam Teeguarden, when she was trying to explain why she thought the linespeople were against her.

Number 9:

"I got tired, my ears started popping, the rubber came off my tennis shoes, I got a cramp, and I lost one of my contact lenses. Other than that, I was in great shape."—Bob Lutz explaining why he just lost his match to Guillermo Vilas.

Number 8:

Frenchman Richard Gasquet, after being suspended for testing positive for cocaine, stated that he actually didn't use the banned substance but simply explained that he kissed a girl who was using cocaine, and that's why he tested positive . . . and the authorities believed him, stating that "The CAS panel decided to dismiss the appeals after having found that in this particular case, Richard Gasquet had not committed any fault or negligence within the meaning of the ITF Anti-Doping Programme." And incredibly, Gasquet was reinstated!

Number 7:

After losing to his countryman, Musumba Bwayla, little-known Zambian pro Lighton Ndefwayl explained his loss as follows: "Bwayla is a stupid man and a hopeless player. He has a huge nose and is cross-eyed. Girls hate him. He beat me because my jockstrap was too tight and because when he serves he farts, and that made me lose my concentration, for which I am famous throughout Zambia."

Number 6:

2012 French Open finalist Sara Errani claimed that she failed a 2017 drug test when the banned substance Letrozole was inadvertently dropped into her tortellini. The ITF tribunal accepted her argument and only gave Errani a light, two-month suspension.

Number 5:

In 2011, Caroline Wozniacki used the following excuse to explain her leg injury: "I saw a kangaroo lying in distress on the grass. Looked so cute, but once it started scratching me, I was a coward and I ran away." But a few hours later, Wozniacki had a change of heart and called another press conference and stated: "I made it up because it sounded better than what actually happened . . . I walked into a treadmill. You know, that's my blonde side. Sometimes that happens."

Number 4:

In 2010, at the Luxembourg Open, top-seeded Elena Dementieva pulled out of the tournament right before her opening round. Her excuse . . . tendinitis in her right foot. Sounds plausible, right? Unfortunately, just four days later, the Russian was running like a thoroughbred at the Doha Masters.

Number 3:

As many tennis fans know, the extremely loud grunting during matches can be off-putting to say the least. But in

June of 2009, when Michelle Larcher de Brito was informed that her vocal cords were more than just a little bit distracting, she retorted with the following: "If they have to fine me, go ahead, because I'd rather get fined than lose a match because I had to stop grunting."

Number 2:

It's never fun when you're playing a match and things aren't going your way. And this statement has never been more apropos than when American Jeff Tarango was losing to Germany's Alexander Mronz of German in the third round of Wimbledon by a score of 6-7, 1-3. As if things weren't bad enough, a crucial call went against Tarango, and let's just say . . . well . . . he lost it! He stormed off the court and accused the chair umpire, Bruno Rebeuh of France, of fixing the match for other players and went on to call the official "corrupt." Sure, Jeff . . . that's why you were losing!

Number 1:

John McEnroe claims he had "temporary insanity" because his wife was pregnant, making him extremely tense, causing him to lose his temper and use obscene language in a third-round match at the U.S. Open in 1987.

Excuses for the Rest of Us

*A*nd just in case you weren't duly inspired by the aforementioned professional excuses, you'll surely find one of the following tried-and-true excuses to fit the bill:

1. I have the worst case of tennis elbow.

Luckily, tennis elbow is something that you feel, but there's no physical sign for your opponent to see. So this is a foolproof excuse that you can use at any time—before, during, or after a match. Typically, though, it will hold the most validity if you have lost the first set, are behind in the second, and you figure you have no chance. Just use a little creativity. How about an "involuntary" cry of pain just after you've hit a backhand, especially if it goes out. Follow this by dramatically dropping your racket, then shaking and rubbing your arm to relieve your agony. It's possible that your opponent is a wannabe doctor who will insist on examining you. If so, simply recoil in pain when he barely touches the top of your forearm.

And there's always the strategy of waiting until the match is over and offering a disingenuous expression of congratulations. Pat his shoulder in a gesture of camaraderie (and if you want to lay it on thick, wince when you use the arm that hurts you) and say, "Good match, buddy. You played great, and I'm pretty sure you probably would have won even if my elbow wasn't killing me."

2. There was a leaf on the court and I couldn't concentrate.

A little bit of OCD never hurts when you're trying to succeed at a difficult task. However, in tennis, having obsessive-compulsive disorder can be about as helpful as having a long tail in a room full of rocking chairs. But if you're looking for a good excuse, a little psychopathology isn't always the worst thing. So after a bad shot, how about getting yourself out of Dodge by uttering, "There was that little annoying leaf on the court, and I couldn't focus at all on the ball." Anyone who has ever needed to wash their hands twice, or line up their silverware, will surely buy such a worthy excuse.

3. The clay court wasn't swept and I kept getting bad bounces.

Have you ever been envious of the pristine conditions at the professional tennis venues? The players get treated like royalty, the prize money can be enormous, and the courts always seem

Did You Know?

Did you know that at the French Open, in order to maintain optimal conditions, the grounds crew sweeps the surface and cleans the lines in between each set? Furthermore, the courts get watered at the end of each match, and again at the end of each day.

to be in perfect condition. But for us weekend warriors, we're left to fend for ourselves. And if you've ever played on public clay courts, you know that they're not exactly like Roland Garros. So the next time the match seems to be going against you, look down at the clay. Pretend to kick at a clump of clay with your foot. And then, when you've been sent home with a big old "L" on your forehead, try out this excuse: "Was it just me, or did that court play really poorly today?"

4. The sun was in my eyes.

A couple of hours on the tennis court can be some of the best moments of one's week. And when the weather is warm, the sky is blue, and there is a cool, refreshing breeze, the experience is only enhanced. But with good weather comes sunshine. And when the match is at its climax, and your opponent throws up a lob, and you look right up into that brightest of celestial objects and literally see stars, you can go from hitting a winner to swinging at the air quicker than a New York minute. And after going from the thrill of victory to the agony of defeat, you can always explain your woeful loss with "That sun was killing me! I might as well have been blindfolded!"

5. I can't play without the proper grip wrap.

Just as a carpenter needs the right tools and an artist needs the right brushes, a tennis player can't be effective without the right equipment. And on that hot, humid day, when your hands are clammy with perspiration and the racket just won't stay properly situated, things can get out of hand (no pun intended) pretty darn quick. So the next time you feel like you're "losing your grip" during a match, you might explain it by stating, "My grip's all wrong. I couldn't hang on to the racket."

Did You Know?

Did you know that in today's modern game, nearly every top player uses a grip wrap to absorb sweat and enhance the feel on the grip?

6. This court is two inches lower than my usual court.

Just as there are no two snowflakes that are identical, there are no two tennis venues that are exactly the same. Some surfaces are harder, softer, faster, slower, more slippery, etc., than others. But in all of my years of playing, one of my favorite all-time excuses for losing is to blame it on something as ridiculous as "The sea level threw off my game." Even if your friends don't buy this excuse, you're sure to get a laugh.

7. I'm much better on hard courts/clay courts/grass courts.

We've all heard it a thousand times: "Variety is the spice of life." But if you ask players like John McEnroe or Pete Sampras, who never solved the mystery of the red clay at the French Open; or Ivan Lendl, who never overcame his aversion to grass at Wimbledon; or even the great Bjorn Borg, who could never win it all on the hard courts of the US Open, you might just get a different response. So if you're one of the many players that specialize on a specific surface, you can shrug off your loss by saying, "This court just doesn't suit my game."

Did You Know?

Did you know that as of the writing of this book, since the beginning of the Open Era, only five men and six women have achieved the career grand slam—winning all four major tournaments (Rod Laver, Andre Agassi, Roger Federer, Rafael Nadal, Novak Djokovic; Margaret Court, Chris Evert, Martina Navratilova, Steffi Graf, Serena Williams, and Maria Sharapova)?

8. My shoes were too tight.

Have you ever heard the joke about the guy who complains about having the same thing for lunch every day? Finally, his coworkers have had enough and say, "Why don't you ask your wife to pack you something different?" Only to have the man reply, "What do you mean? I pack my own lunch." But here's an excuse you can use over and over (as long as it's not with the same opponent): "My shoes were killing me!"

9. My opponent was a pusher.

You wouldn't hire a plumber who can't fix a leaky faucet. Nor would you choose a doctor who says, "I can't help you if you're really sick." But somehow, in tennis it's a perfectly valid excuse to state that you can't play well against a specific

Did You Know?

Did you know that Chris Evert, whom many pundits consider a pusher, won 18 Grand Slam singles titles and is widely thought of as one of the greatest players of all time?

playing style. So the next time you go down to defeat, you might want to try this one on for size: "My opponent was a pusher . . . The only reason I lost is that I just don't enjoy playing that kind of game." Odds are that most of your buddies will be nodding their heads in agreement.

10. I was distracted by my opponent's grunting.

Tennis has historically been a game played by ladies and gentlemen who adhered to the rules of etiquette. From

Did You Know?

Did you know that there was such a backlash against Monica Seles, one of the most famous "grunters" of all time, that she actually played one of her most important matches, her only Wimbledon Final, in near silence and lost 6-2, 6-1 to Steffi Graf?

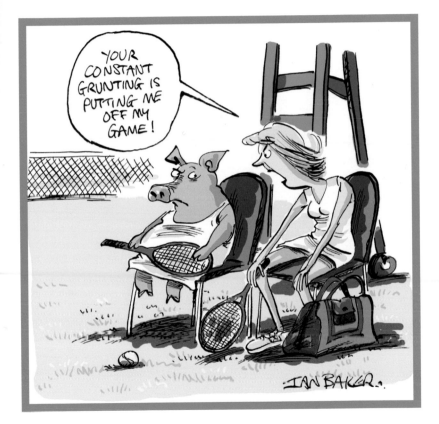

proper manners to lily-white attire, tennis had always been a game of nobility. But players such as Nastase, Connors, McEnroe, and Agassi changed all of that. With flash and brash, these tennis pioneers put some spice into a previously pretty bland recipe. I think most of us would agree that the result has been an improved product, but while vocal crowds and flamboyant outfits may now be widely accepted, one thing that is still frowned upon is shrieking in the middle of points. So after a bad loss, most players will sympathize if you say, "That guy was screaming every time he took a swing. How do you concentrate when your opponent sounds like a moose in heat?"

11. I skipped church this week, and God is getting even with me.

We've all heard it stated by the world's best athletes: "All the glory of a monumental win goes to the Good Lord above." "It was due to God's will that I came out victorious." "Thank you Lord for this most glorious achievement." Yet I've never quite understood why today's athletic elite believe that God only plays a role when you win. So the next time you are dealt a crushing blow, how about trying, "I didn't pray this week, and God held it against me."

12. Sweat got into my eyes.

When you're in the heat of competition, everyone knows that you need to give 110 percent. Without a full physical and mental effort, a difficult win is going to be nearly impossible. And like everything in life, the best achievements are worth working for. But when you give your best effort and running at a full sprint for every shot, something interesting tends to occur . . . you may actually perspire a bit. So an obvious excuse would be "My headband couldn't stop the sweat in my eyes. You know how it is. You can't hit what you can't see."

13. My opponent was hooking me.

Sometimes in tennis, as in life, you get off to a great start only to have the wheels fall off. How could it be that you

can be dominating a match, only to fall apart and have your opponent make a comeback and snatch away your victory? If this most unfortunate of circumstances is to occur, and you can't figure out why your near victory turned into a crushing defeat, you can always state, "I was about to win but that guy started making terrible calls and stole the match from me."

> ### Did You Know?
>
> *Did you know that in the 1972 Davis Cup Final between Romania and the United States, played in Bucharest, Romania, the linespeople were blatantly giving favorable calls to the home team? Despite the obvious cheating, the United States prevailed 3 matches to 2.*

14. The lighting was poor.

As has been said, seeing is believing. But if you can't see that little yellow fuzzy ball clearly, I'm sure you will believe that you're likely to lose the match. So the next time you lose that late-afternoon match as the sun is beginning to set, you might actually feel justified in uttering, "It was just too dark to see the ball clearly. We should have called it off and finished tomorrow."

15. I lost a contact lens.

You can lose a lot of things in life . . . your keys, your concentration, your self-confidence, etc. So if you ask me, it's a completely valid excuse to say, "Can you believe it? That little contact lens popped out of my eye, and it cost me the match."

16. The weather was horrible.

As any weatherman worth their salt will tell you, the right conditions can make all the difference. Whether you're on vacation, or simply taking a walk around the block, everyone wants to feel comfortable. So when the outside elements aren't ideal, why not tell anyone who will listen, "The weather was awful. That's what cost me that match."

Did You Know?

Did you know that many tournaments now have an "Extreme Heat Policy" where play is halted (or if applicable, a retractable roof is closed) when the heat becomes so unbearable that it's dangerous to the players?

17. My glasses were dirty.

"Cleanliness is next to Godliness." How many times did you hear that one growing up? And although I freely admit that there are times when rolling around in the mud and getting filled with grime and mud can be exhilarating, most tennis players try to avoid getting filthy during their matches. So for those spectacled weekend warriors out there, an excuse of "I couldn't see! A spot of dirt got on my glasses during a critical point and I couldn't get it off" could be appropriate. That might just be what the ophthalmologist ordered.

18. It was too windy.

There's nothing like a nice, calm summer breeze to refresh the soul of a warm summer day. But there is also something to be said for moderation. So the next time those Santa Ana winds come a blowin', you might want to tell everyone who will listen, "The tennis ball looked more like a ping pong ball dancing in the wind."

19. I've never seen my opponent play that well.

Tennis can be the most fickle of paramours. You can have a day where you aren't at your best and still come out on top. But of course, as we all know, there are days when your opponent seems to just never miss a shot. So the next time your reliable punching bag punches back a little harder, and you end up on the losing side of the stick, you can explain it by simply stating, "He was playing out of his mind!"

Did You Know?

Did you know that in 1987, after the man-child phenom Boris Becker had won back-to-back Wimbledon titles as a teenager, he was upset by 70th-ranked Peter Doohan of Australia? After the match, Becker was quoted as saying, "I just did not think he was that good."

20. The players from the next court kept hitting their balls onto our court.

One of the reasons why tennis is such a fantastic sport is that it is not only a test of one's physical abilities, but of one's mental side, as well. It takes a complete body and mind effort to pull off a difficult victory. So don't you just hate it when the balls from the neighboring court continuously interrupt your match? It can be so darn distracting! But in the world of the best tennis excuses, playing on the public courts with balls flying at you from every direction might just be an asset. Because the next time you have amateurs playing on either side of you, your loss can be explained by stating, "The balls coming from the next court drove me crazy."

21. That guy was so darn lucky!

"Better to be lucky than good." And not so great when the luck is on the other side of the net. So when every net-cord and line clipper seem to go against you, an excuse of "That lucky stiff!" might just be warranted.

22. These tennis balls are too fast/slow/heavy/ light/fuzzy/bald/soft/hard.

There are several different brands and types of tennis balls, but what happens if the one you're using isn't up to standards? You guessed it, a ball that is out of kilter can cause a shot that usually lands two inches inside—or outside—of the court. The next time you find your shots slightly askew, try telling your comrades, "Something's wrong with that ball!" Any football fan who was following the Deflategate scandal, where the New England Patriots were accused of using footballs that were slightly deflated in order to gain an unfair advantage, will surely understand.

Did You Know?

Did you know that in professional tennis, new balls are used after the first seven games, and then every nine games after that? (The warm-up is thought to count as two games worth of usage.)

23. I'm not used to this racket.

Many players grow to love and rely on their most coveted weapon like Linus from *Peanuts* relies on his blanket . . . it's that familiar friend that's always there for you. But what happens when the time comes to make a change? As technology improves, a favorite weapon may need to be exchanged for a new best friend. But if you've recently made a change, and the end result ends up being a loss, you can always use the time-honored, "I need more time to get used to my new stick."

24. I just couldn't focus.

If you want to play tennis at a top level, the task at hand needs your undivided concentration. So if you've recently squabbled with your significant other, or had a bad day at work, you might just be able to use that unfortunate set of events to explain why you lost the match: "Couldn't concentrate. My mind was all over the place."

25. I went out last night drinking, and now I'm hungover.

If you are one of the countless weekend warriors reading this book, the next time you are out with your comrades tossing back a drink or two, and then have to get up the next morning for that early Saturday or Sunday match, this excuse may just be for you. If your head is pounding and your stomach is churning and you end up on the wrong side of the scoreboard, you might want to explain it by stating, "I was so hungover that I consider it a victory that I didn't throw up on myself during the match."

Did You Know?

Did you know that before the Open Era, the professional players used to travel, fraternize, and even party together before their matches?

26. My sunglasses kept slipping off of my nose.

This excuse works best if you have one of those cute, petite noses that every plastic surgeon admires. The next time you find yourself in a deep hole down a set and a break, and it's a sunny day, shake your head a little harder than normal now and again. And when your sunglasses fall to the ground, sigh loudly about how the gosh darn glasses need to be adjusted. And after the inevitable loss, when you're shaking hands at the net, you might want to try uttering, "I really need to get to the ophthalmologist, these glasses just won't do."

27. My tennis shorts are too tight.

There is nothing like a nice, tight outfit on a weekend night to attract a little attention. But on the tennis court, your snug shorts might just cause a pain in the behind. So the next time you feel like you're about to split your seams, how about quoting Judge Smails from *Caddyshack*: "It's easy to grin when your ship comes in, and you've got the stock market beat, but the man worthwhile is the man who can smile, when his short are too tight in the seat!"

28. I broke a string and didn't have another racket.

Ya gotta be a boy scout: "Be prepared." But what happens if your favorite (and only) weapon pops a string in the middle of a point? Perfect time for the excuse: "If it weren't for bad luck, I'd have no luck at all. That broken string cost me the match."

Did You Know?

Did you know that in a second-round match at the 2000 Samsung Open against Hjung-Taik Lee of South Korea, Goran Ivanisevic had to default his match after he ran out of rackets? The umpire announced the default because of a "lack of appropriate equipment."

29. I was just so inconsistent.

Slow and steady wins the race. But what happens when your backhand just seems to fly outside of the lines, or when your net game is nonexistent? Don't even think of admitting that your opponent is better than you.

Start off by making a gesture of disgust when you miss a shot, then follow that up with some verbal outbursts, and when it becomes inevitable that you're going to lose, forget about showing any class. After all, would you rather lose with

Did You Know?

Did you know that Yevgeny Kafelnikov holds the record for the most unforced errors at a Grand Slam singles match with 112 while playing Fernando Vicente at the 2000 French Open . . . and incredibly still won the match?!

dignity, or offer some kind of excuse, no matter how lame? For purposes of this discussion, let's assume that you're not going to take the high road. In that case, no problem. Just shrug nonchalantly and say, "I guess you can claim a win if you want to, but man, was I inconsistent today."

30. I need more lessons.

Practice makes perfect. So the next time you're not playing up to snuff, and you can't seemingly remember how to hit the ball within the white lines, how about explaining your woeful play to your compatriots with "If I just had more lessons, I surely would have won."

31. I shouldn't have eaten right before the match.

When it's obvious that you're going to lose, a sudden attack of nausea can come in handy; maybe you can even fake a retch or two. You can then call off the match due to illness and thereby claim that your opponent didn't actually win because "I shouldn't have had that greasy hamburger for lunch."

32. I never served this badly.

We've all had our bad days. Some days your kids just drive you crazy. On others your significant other might be giving you a hard time. Or perhaps you just woke up on the wrong side of the bed. So why can't things go badly on the tennis court, as well? And is there any worse feeling when you can't even start off the point with a decent serve?! It can truly throw off your entire game. So the next time you toss in a double fault or two, you can explain the loss with "My serve has never, ever been so pathetic."

33. My backhand let me down.

Claiming that your elbow was painful when you switched to the backhand side can lend a bit of legitimacy to your

otherwise lame excuse. A sudden cry of agony when you miss a down-the-line backhand will also bolster your case. How about "I can't believe it. My backhand's normally my best shot."

Did You Know?

Did you know that Jimmy Connors, who had one of the best backhands of all time, never won the French Open, a tournament where one's ground strokes are the key to winning the event?!

34. I got the worst cramp.

As any top player can tell you, conditioning is an essential part of the game. And as many weekend warriors can surely attest, their physical attributes may not quite be up to herculean standards. So the next time you're playing on a hot day, and you're down in the third set, you might want to try "This cramp is killing me!" It just might do the trick.

Did You Know?

Did you know that at the US Open in 1995, Shuzo Matsuoka from Japan was left writhing in pain after severely cramping in his first round match against Petr Korda? The heinous incident led to a rules change that now allows professional players to receive medical treatment for cramps during their matches.

35. My usual stringer is on vacation.

When using this excuse, be sure to tap your strings frequently and at the same time put on an expression of confusion when you listen to the sound. Also spend a lot of time readjusting the strings, especially when you miss a shot. When your opponent isn't looking, you can also remove the vibration damper, put it in your pocket, and take several minutes pretending to look for it all over the court. And if all else fails, smashing your racket on the fence post in frustration can come in handy, followed by "I'm not playing again until my stringer gets back home."

Did You Know?

Did you know that many of the elite tennis players actually have their own personal racket stringers travel with them around the world just to get that perfect string tension?

36. I've got a bad back.

This one is pure gold. Back pain is one of the most common ailments known to athletes and nonathletes alike. And consequently, many of us know what it's like to lie on a hard floor without moving a muscle, just hoping the pain will go away. A bad back can be at the least a nuisance, and at times even debilitating. But why not use your back pain to your advantage? The next time you lose because you can't quite get low enough to reach that drop shot, or can't quite reach up high enough for that overhead smash, just take the wind out of your opponent's sails: "Congratulations. I'll let you know when my back spasms let up so we can have a better game next time."

Did You Know?

Did you know that Andre Agassi's back was so bad during the end of his career that he used to endure painful injections to numb the pain before his matches in order to play?

37. I'm usually much better.

Berating yourself frequently during your match can be effective here, such as screaming your own name when you flub a shot, then "Come on! Watch the ball! Concentrate! What's the matter with you?"

Follow this with a lot of pouting, and then say to your opponent while shaking your head sadly, "Sorry, I was trying to give you some competition, but I just don't have it today."

38. I had an off day.

We've all awakened on the wrong side of the bed from time to time. We get a bad night's sleep. We can't seem to concentrate. The list goes on and on. It can affect our work, our relationships, and, you guessed it . . . even our tennis game. So an excuse of "I was just off today" is as valid a reason as any for finding yourself on the losing end of a match.

39. My opponent's tennis outfit distracted me.

This could apply to lots of situations: You're a guy, playing a girl, and she's wearing a very short skirt with frilly panties. Or you're playing another guy and you can't believe he's beating you because he's dressed in rags. Or your regular opponent shows up in a brand-new outfit, all the way down to new shoes and socks. You figure it must be his birthday; otherwise, why would he be so confident to wear something so attention-getting? In any case, you're distracted, so it just can't be your fault if you're on the wrong end of the score. When walking off the court after a loss, be sure to say something like, "What the heck is with that outfit you're wearing today? If I didn't know better, I'd think you dressed that way just to throw me off."

Did You Know?

Did you know that in the first round at Wimbledon in 1985, where the rules state that a player must wear white tennis attire, Anne White wore a lycra white bodysuit in her match against Pam Shriver? When the match was stopped at one set each due to darkness, the umpire, Alan Mills, told White to wear more appropriate clothing the next day . . . White complied and lost the match.

40. I broke a shoelace.

If Tanya Harding can break a lace on her ice skate and use it as a valid excuse in the Olympics, it will surely pass muster on the tennis court. I mean, how can you be expected to perform at your best if you don't have the proper footwork? In my opinion, it's an underutilized excuse but a good one: "My shoelace broke and completely messed up my footwork."

41. I forgot my wristband.

This one applies only on hot, humid days, or if you normally sweat a lot despite the weather. To be sure you have this to rely on, don't start off wearing a wristband, even if you have several in your bag. Then, when you're losing, start to complain about your hand and wrist being too sweaty, and while your opponent isn't looking, pretend to be unable to find a wristband. Of course, this could backfire if your opponent then offers you one of his. In this case, you will actually have to try to win the match. In any case, be sure to mention that once your grip was wet, you were unable to recover your concentration.

42. My headband was too tight.

One of the many reasons I love tennis is that it's not just a game of physical prowess, but it's a mental battle, as well. We all know the supertalented player who just can't seem to keep it together between the ears. The next time you lose concentration, try letting your opponent know that "I had to use a headband today, but it was so tight that it cut off the circulation to my brain."

43. My knee brace broke.

It's rather unlikely for your knee brace to actually break, but your opponent doesn't need to know that. Once you're sure you're going to lose, start fidgeting with the brace and put on an expression of impatience and frustration. Then angrily rip off the brace, throw it to the ground, curse your orthopedist and the brace's manufacturer, and begin to limp pathetically. You don't need to fall to the ground, however. Just collapsing into a chair and looking disgusted will work every time. Follow this with "Can you believe that 200-dollar knee brace fell apart? They just don't make stuff like they used to."

If you can pull this off, your opponent might even feel sorry for you and offer to buy you a beer.

44. I have a blister.

We've all had them, and it can be oh so painful. A blister on your hand or foot can make it hard to perform even the most menial of tasks. And because so many of us know what it's like to suffer this way, an excuse of "I have a blister and am simply in too much pain to play at my best" will surely be met with unbridled sympathy and turn what could have been a humiliating loss into a get-well-soon card.

45. I have athlete's foot.

This is a tough one. You'll have to squirm around in your shoes for a while, meanwhile complaining about itching and soreness in your feet. Taking off your shoes and rubbing your toes through your socks can be somewhat convincing, and keeping a can of some kind of powder in your bag can also help to support your case. But never allow your opponent to look at your feet, even if he's a podiatrist. Just tell him it's too embarrassing and say, "Man, I can't believe how my athlete's foot screwed up my game."

46. It's too humid.

I think we can all agree that tennis is a terrific game . . . but nobody ever said that it was easy. And one of the things that can make this sport so difficult is the ever-changing elements. The sun, the wind, the cold, you name it and tennis can throw it at you. But despite the fact that everyone knows that the elements are part of the game, it's still a very valid excuse to blame the conditions. And on those days where the air just seems to be filled with water, why not try "It was just so humid . . . I could barely breathe!"

47. My strings are too tight.

Many of tennis's powerful players like tight strings. A high string tension can add control to your game. And although you'll sacrifice power, keeping the ball in the court may just outweigh that decrease in the pop on your shots. But if you're playing a speedster, and you just can't get the ball past him, why not blame the loss on your stringer? Let your opponent know that "These strings are just way too tight. I feel like Samson after a trip to his barber. I've simply lost all of my power."

48. My strings are too loose.

As most astute tennis players know, when your strings are too loose, you sacrifice control. Sure, you get a little more pop on your shots, but a heck of a lot of good that will do you when you are spraying the ball like an aerosol can. The next time you are crushing the ball like a Greek god only to have your efforts end up far outside the lines, let your opponent know that "My strings are just way too loose."

49. There were people walking behind the court.

You can fall back on this one when it's obvious that you're
going to lose, and you can't think of anything else. Make a
big display of annoyance at those who are passing by, shrug
and spread your arms in a gesture of disbelief, and stop for
a prolonged time until they pass. And if you really want to
milk it, hold up your hand to your opponent to halt play and
ask if he knows who they were because you want to confront
them. Then, when the match is over, make a comment like
"Can you believe how inconsiderate those people were? We
had a good match going and then I completely lost my concentration when they were walking by!"

50. There was too much noise.

I never fully understood why tennis players require silence
during play. Sure, I get that it takes absolute concentration
and precision to play at a top level. But doesn't it also take a
huge mental effort to throw a 95-mile-an-hour fastball in the

bottom of the ninth inning? Or doesn't it also take all the skill and focus one can muster to lead your team down a football field with two minutes left in the fourth quarter? Yet these athletes seem to perform with the crowd in a fury. But the rules of tennis etiquette are clear, and silence is required. So the next time you're playing at your club, or at the park courts, and you hear some incidental outside noise, why not use it to your advantage and let your opponent know that "I just couldn't play at my best with all of that distracting noise."

51. I stubbed my toe.

The first step for this excuse is to let out a loud "Ouch!" while chasing down a ball that's out of your reach. Then stop suddenly and hop around on one foot, followed by a minute or so of pathetic limping. Taking off your shoe and rubbing your big toe will also help to authenticate your contrived drama, but to prove your toughness, soldier on like a martyr and continue playing until the bitter end. Then, when the match is over, sit down heavily and remove your shoe again. (Caution: Be sure you take off the same shoe!) And this time, pull off your stinky sock, as well. Wave it around a bit so your opponent can get a good whiff, and say, "Geez, I really stubbed this toe. Would you mind taking a close look to see if it's injured?" If you keep that foul-smelling sock nearby, chances are he'll take your word for it.

52. I thought it was first ball in.

Like in all sports, getting off to a good start is essential. And after a quick warm-up period, it's time to get started. In this case, it's important to use your excuse right away. If you unfortunately start off with a double fault, turn that inopportune event into a more than valid excuse by stating, "That shouldn't be a double fault because I thought it was first ball in."

53. My opponent's phone kept ringing, and it threw off my concentration.

It's bound to happen. In today's go, go, go world, it seems like we always need to be connected. And it can actually be quite annoying. You're trying to enjoy a couple of hours of peace and quiet on the tennis court, and your opponent's phone won't stop ringing. Well, why not use this to your advantage? If you go down in flames, hit your opponent with the following: "You really impressed me today. I can't believe how well you played with your cell phone ringing off the hook. Personally, I couldn't concentrate with all that ringing . . . but kudos to you."

54. I didn't have time to properly warm up.

The warm-up period for a tennis match is usually pretty quick. For example, in the pros they only have a five-minute window

Did You Know?

Did you know that even though the professionals only have five minutes to warm up before their matches, they spend hours preparing to play before they actually walk onto the court?

before the match gets under way. And in my experience, the weekend warriors generally follow suit. But this is something you can use to your advantage. The next time your opponent is rushing you to get the match started, you can let anyone who will listen know that "Next time we play I'm not going to let him rush me through the warm-up. By the time I got loose the match was over."

55. It's too dark.

Sometimes Mother Nature will come to the rescue when things aren't going your way on the court. Let's say it's springtime, the days are getting longer, and you're trying to get in an evening match before the sun goes down. You're loving the crisp air and playing well, but then your opponent turns the tables and pulls ahead. You've never lost to him/her before, and you don't want to spoil that record. No need to panic. Now's the time to put on the brakes. Slow down the pace of play, start a prolonged argument about the score or a line call, pretend to hear your cell phone ring and fake a long conversation. There are surely lots of other ploys. Just use your imagination, and if you play your cards right it's a no-brainer. After you've pushed it to the limit, glance at your watch, put on a sympathetic face, and say, "Gee, what a shame. You were playing so well, but I guess we have to call it on account of darkness."

56. I can't play well when people are watching me.

Performance anxiety is a real thing. Ask anyone whose mind has ever gone blank during an exam, or anyone who has ever . . . uh-hem . . . had difficulty in the bedroom. And performance anxiety is a major part of "freezing up" in sports. Whether it's extra innings in a baseball game, overtime in basketball or football, or a third-set tiebreaker, anxiety can interfere with optimal performance. But many of us really panic when people are watching us. It's one thing to play a match on an outer court when it's just you, your opponent, and your thoughts. But what happens if you're on one of the show courts with five, ten, or even twenty people watching? If that's the case, and you crack under the added pressure, try telling people, "I simply can't play my best when I'm being watched."

Did You Know?

Did you know that the most widely viewed tennis match of all time may shock you? It was the **2011 Women's French Open Final where Chinese superstar Li Na defeated Francesca Schiavone 6-4, 7-6.** Incredibly, in China alone there were said to be **116 million viewers,** and possibly as many as **330 million viewers worldwide.**

57. I never play this badly.

This one is an oldie but a goodie. You're playing against a clearly superior opponent. Let's be honest, you couldn't beat this player if your life depended on it. And after your opponent has mopped up the court with you, let them know that "I really have never played this poorly." Most people will know that you're just blowing smoke, but at least it will make you feel better."

58. I need a new racket.

The right equipment is essential for playing your best. And as every tennis player knows, your most important tool is your racket. Technology is always changing, and rackets are constantly getting lighter, and more powerful with better control. If you haven't updated your weapon in a while, let anyone who will listen know that "If I only had a new racket, I surely would have played better."

59. I need new shoes.

Ideally, this excuse should be planned in advance. When you're scheduled to play an opponent who's sure to beat you, dig an old pair of sneakers out of your closet and wrap a lot of black tape around the toes. During the match, hobble a little between points, retie the laces several times, bang the shoes with your racket as if you're trying to make them more comfortable, and during change of sides, take one shoe off and shake it as though there were a stone inside. When no stone emerges, hold the shoe up, peer inside, and then stretch it as though you were changing its shape. When you have been soundly thrashed, even a cynic will sympathize when you whine pathetically, "Man, I wish I could afford a new pair of shoes. These things felt like they were going to fall off today."

60. I need a new outfit.

To look good is to feel good. And to feel good is to be at your best, both mentally and physically. Therefore, it goes without saying that if you want to play your best tennis, you clearly need to look the part. If you come out on the losing side of your weekend matchup, try uttering, "I needed a better outfit to play at my best."

61. My racket is too old.

We all know the player who is always trying to buy a better game. One week they show up with new shoes, the next week it's a new wristband. In reality, I believe that it doesn't matter if you have the most expensive equipment if you can't hit a good shot to save your life. But that doesn't mean that you can't use this excuse to your advantage. If you're down and out, start to look closely at your racket. You might even want to ask your opponent if they can hear the strange rattling sound your racket is making. Then, after the match, try smoothly telling your opponent, "You played great today. It's amazing I even won a point with this old, broken-down racket."

Did You Know?

Did you know that for many years, tennis rackets were made of laminated wood, and a wooden racket was even used at Wimbledon as late as 1987? However, in today's modern game, most rackets are made of a composite of high-tech metals.

62. I started off slowly.

In any sport, it's essential to get off to a fast start. Don't believe me? Just ask Usain Bolt how important it is to get out of the blocks quickly in his 100-meter races. Or ask the pitcher who gives up three runs in the first inning, only to have his team lose by a run at the end of the game. Well, the same thing is true on the tennis court. If you start out slowly, you might end up behind the eight ball for the entire match. The next time your serve gets broken in the first game, and your opponent ends up dominating from there, try this one on for size: "My slow start doomed my performance."

63. I have the worst headache.

When it becomes obvious that you have no chance to win, slow down between points, place your hand over your eyes, and shake your head pathetically. When your opponent asks if you're okay, just wave him off and soldier on for a few points. Then, when you're between games, press your fingers to your temples and say, "Sorry, I can't finish the match. My head's killing me."

64. I'm too old/fat/short/slow.

Blaming your physical physique for losing a tennis match is like blaming your low IQ for doing poorly on the SATs . . . well, no duh you lost, you're completely out of shape. Yet somehow, in this great sport of ours, it is completely acceptable to blame a loss on a lack of physical prowess. It

---

Did You Know?

Did you know that during the 1973 Battle of the Sexes match, fifty-five-year-old Bobby Riggs told everyone who would listen that he would surely easily dispatch of Billie Jean King, who was twenty-six years his junior, because, as Riggs put it, female players were inferior to men? King won the match 6-4, 6-3, 6-3, and it is widely heralded as a landmark event in the history of parity in sports.

therefore goes without saying that the next time you're up against a clearly superior athlete, try letting your competitor know: "Sorry. My game wasn't what it should be. Too many people depending on me at work and home, so no time to get into top shape."

65. I need a new coach.

The pros do it all the time. And not just in tennis. In any sport I can think of, when a player or team struggles, the coach is normally the first one to get the ax. So why should it matter that you're simply a weekend warrior? If you find yourself on a losing streak, or even if you just need that perfect excuse for the right moment, let anyone in earshot know

Did You Know?

Did you know that tennis is one of the only sports where coaching is not allowed during the actual competition?

"It's time for a new coach . . . my current guy simply hasn't evolved with my ever-changing game."

66. There were no windscreens.

The strategy here is to lose on purpose! (But only when it becomes obvious that you're going to lose anyway.) Start to grumble that the wind is throwing you off, and then intentionally hit the ball too wide or too long, depending on the direction of the wind. If it's blowing from the side, aim just outside the opposite sideline so that the wind will help to carry it out for sure. And if it's coming from behind you, shoot for beyond the opponent's baseline so that the ball will go long.

But what if there's no wind?, you might ask. No problem. Complain that you're near-sighted and you have no depth perception without the backdrop of windscreens.

In either case, your excuse will be easy: "I can't believe these cheap SOBs won't spring for windscreens. I can't play decent tennis under such lousy conditions."

67. When I lost the coin toss, the momentum shifted against me.

Sometimes it's just one of those days. The longer you play, the worse you get, and there's just no fixing it. So when you've lost, take away your opponent's satisfaction by commenting, "I had no karma today. I knew it when you won the serve on the coin toss."

68. I've recently had surgery.

The definition of surgery can be quite broad, so if you're desperate, you can pull this one out of your bag of tricks to explain why you lost. After the match, sit quietly for a while and put on a pensive expression until your opponent asks if you're okay. Then flick your hand in a dismissive motion and mumble something about a health problem. Chances are he'll express sympathy and ask what's wrong. At this point, it's critically important to maintain that pensive expression. Above all, remain evasive and never give a clear answer. I would suggest something like "Well, I really don't want to talk about it, but I never should have tried to play this soon after having surgery."

(He doesn't need to know your "surgery" was a visit to the dentist two weeks ago to have your teeth cleaned.)

> ### Did You Know?
>
> Did you know that American male tennis player Richard Raskind underwent sex reassignment surgery and later played on the women's tour as Renée Richards?

69. I had a big fight with my husband/wife/boss/children/parents, and now I can't concentrate.

A lot of my tennis friends have told me that they love playing tennis because it completely frees up their minds from all of their other worries. And when a player can solely focus on the task at hand, they increase their odds of playing at the highest level. But what happens when you've got troubles on your mind? Well, I say use this to your advantage, as well. Whether it was a huge blowout with your spouse,

or your boss simply asked you to work on a Saturday . . . or if you've got no troubles whatsoever, and you simply need a good excuse . . . it will be our secret. After a humiliating loss, let 'em know, "Right before the match I had a huge fight and I just couldn't concentrate."

> ## Did You Know?
> *Did you know that despite John McEnroe's legendary temper outbursts, he won seven Grand Slam singles titles and is considered to be one of the most talented players to ever pick up a racket?*

70. I thought we were playing with no-ad scoring.

The scoring in tennis can be a little tricky. While everyone knows a baseball game is nine innings and a football game is sixty minutes, you generally need to determine how long your match is going to be ahead of time. Are you going to play 2 out of 3 sets or 3 out of 5? Are you going to play a standard set or an eight-game pro set? And of course there is the question of playing with ad scoring or without. So the next time you lose a pivotal deuce game, you can explain the loss with, "I thought we were playing with no-ad scoring. I'm much better when the pressure is on."

71. I forgot my sunscreen.

You'll have to save this one for a sunny day. As soon as you begin to fall behind in a match, repeatedly glance upward at the sky, squint as you do so, and start to examine the skin on your arms. Then, between games, show your opponent a freckle that's been there since you were born. "Look at this! Can you believe it? I forgot my sunscreen." Then, with a worried expression: "Do you think I need to see a dermatologist?" But be prepared if he offers you some sunscreen of his own. "Thanks, but I need stuff with a protection rating of 'x'" (at least a level or two above his).

Seek out shade between games, and if there's a shadow near the fence, hang out there while your opponent is picking up balls on his side. And when it's over, and you have once more gone down in flames, "Sorry. Couldn't keep my mind on the game. After all, there's nothing more important than good health, right?"

72. It was so bright out, I couldn't see the ball.

There's nothing quite like a nice, bright, summertime day. While the glare of the bright sun might make for perfect beach weather, it can be pure misery on the court. The next time you catch yourself squinting to see the ball, tell your opponent, "It was too bright, and I just couldn't get a good look at the ball."

73. I didn't stretch out properly before the match.

Don't worry if you didn't actually forget to stretch prior to playing. Your opponent doesn't know that. Simply start by walking stiffly. And make sure to struggle when you bend over to pick up the balls. In between games, you'll want to make a mock attempt to stretch, but of course it will be in vain . . . your body is just too tight now. After the inevitable loss, make sure to say something like "You played really well; if I had only remembered to stretch out before the match, I probably could have given you my best."

74. My opponent was taking too much time between points, and it completely threw off my timing.

Per rule number 29, a player is only allowed 20 seconds between points at Grand Slams (25 seconds for other ATP events). However, this rule is rarely enforced. But that doesn't mean you can't use it to your advantage. The next time you find your opponent lollygagging between points, and to make matters worse you're getting the stuffing beaten out of you, try stating, "That guy I was playing kept breaking the rules by taking way too much time between points. I couldn't possibly get into my normal rhythm."

75. My girlfriend/boyfriend was watching, and I was so nervous.

As anyone who has ever picked up a racket can attest, tennis is a hard enough game on a typical day. But what happens if that boy or girl whom you fancy just happens to be watching you play? The added pressure can be devastating. But if your significant other is nearby, use this knowledge wisely and let your opponent know "My boyfriend/girlfriend was watching, and I felt so much pressure that I couldn't play my best."

76. I was distracted by the hottie sitting courtside.

Let's face it, we're all human. And sometimes, no matter how young or old we are, or how much we love our significant other, it's just natural to find a good-looking person attractive. The next time you see a supercute man or woman sitting next to the court, and you can't take your eyes off of them, try uttering, "I couldn't focus at all with that smoking hot creature sitting so close to my match."

77. I was up late last night and was too sleepy to play well.

As good old Ben Franklin could tell you, "Early to bed and early to rise makes a man healthy, wealthy, and wise." There's a lot of wisdom in this quote, and it holds true on the tennis court, as well. And to make this excuse even better, everybody knows how tough it is to function when you haven't slept well . . . so use it to your advantage. If you find yourself down in a match, start to yawn a lot and rub your eyes. Begin mumbling about how tired you are, and after the match simply state, "I just had the worst night's sleep and I'm exhausted."

78. The shot was so easy that I lost my focus.

Sometimes in life, what seems like the easiest of tasks can actually be quite difficult. This is true whether you're taking part in a routine task, or if you're on the tennis court. The next time you have a sitter overhead that you butcher like a pork chop, it can be quite embarrassing. But before your cheeks get redder than your Christmas lights, simply explain it by saying, "I blew that shot because I lost my focus. It was just too easy."

79. I was so much better than my opponent that I was overconfident.

It sounds like a line out of *Star Wars*, but just as a Jedi Knight might tell his apprentice, "Your overconfidence is your downfall," the same can be said in tennis. You have to

> ### Did You Know?
>
> Did you know that in the semifinals of the 2015 US Open, Serena Williams was on her way to becoming only the third women's player in the Open Era to achieve a calendar year Grand Slam—after Margaret Smith Court in 1970 and Steffi Graff in 1988—when she lost to the Italian Roberta Vinci in what is widely considered to be one of the biggest upsets in the history of tennis?

take every opponent seriously. But what happens when you are clearly the better player, and you just know you are going to win . . . until you lose, that is? In a case such as this, you can simply say, "I was like young Skywalker. My overconfidence did me in."

80. My coach told me how well I've been playing recently and jinxed me.

Anyone reading this book a bit superstitious? Well, if you're a sports fan, you just might be. And at times, a "jinx" can mean the difference between winning and losing. As George Costanza might say from *Seinfeld*, "It's only a jinx if you believe it." The next time you pay an arm and a leg for lessons, and end up in defeat despite the hard-earned money spent, how about trying "My coach told me how well I was playing recently and completely put the hex on me."

81. I didn't think the ball was going to come over the net.

As any good boy scout will tell you, always be prepared. But sometimes, in sports, and for that matter in life, we let our guard down just a bit, and it can come back to bite us right in the . . . well, you know where. On that next big point, when things don't go your way, try "I wasn't ready for that dinky shot. Couldn't believe it came over the net."

82. I didn't think the shot was going in.

In sports, at times, the contest can be completely one-sided. However, it can also come down to the final point. If you find yourself in a nail-biter, and lose at the very end, you can summarize your defeat with "I didn't think that last shot was going in, and it cost me the match."

83. I had a bad draw.

Even the top professionals will tell you that they like to ease their way into a tournament. And a couple of easy rounds can be just the ticket. But what happens when you draw a top player in the first or second round? Your dreams of a late tournament run might be dashed before you get out of the starting gate. The next time you lose in the first or second round of your club tournament, you can always explain it by saying, "I got a bad deal in this tournament. If I had had a better draw, I would have gone a lot deeper."

84. I didn't play at my best.

We all have off days at times. Perhaps you have a headache, a stiff back, a lot of stress at work . . . or maybe you just woke up on the wrong side of the bed. Everyone can relate. That's what makes this excuse so good. The next time you need a run-of-the-mill, generic excuse that is sure to do the trick, try "I simply had an off day and didn't play up to my normal standards."

85. I felt sluggish and couldn't get going.

We've all felt it when we weren't at our best. When we woke up on the wrong side of the bed, or we simply couldn't get our juices flowing. The next time you are out late and then have to wake up for an early match, or when you eat a big lunch right before your early afternoon encounter, how about saying, "Just didn't have any energy today. Threw off my entire game."

86. I didn't prepare my equipment as carefully as I should have.

As my father often taught me, preparation is half the battle. If you prepare well, you're sure to increase your chances of success. And tennis is no different. From a good grip wrap to the right string job, no detail is too small to overlook. So how about letting your opponent know "My equipment simply let me down." It's as worthy an excuse as any other.

87. It was too cold.

I ask you, dear reader, is there anything better than playing a match bathed in the warm sunshine of a pleasant summer's day? But for many of us, waiting until the warm months to play our beloved sport just isn't an option. The next time you go out to swat a couple of forehands and backhands on a blustery fall day, and you end up on the wrong side of the scoreboard, I believe a more than valid excuse is "An Eskimo would have struggled to play well on a day as cold as this."

88. I played too aggressively.

Sometimes in sports you have to go for the throat . . . go for the kill . . . swing for the knockout punch. But if you're one of those players who plays full throttle at all times, and end up making five times as many errors as winners, just let your opponent know, "I played way too aggressively, and it cost me the match." This should do the trick.

89. I played too conservatively.

I've heard it mentioned many times throughout my life in sports—No guts, no glory. Sometimes you just have to go for it! But what happens when you're just too afraid to make errors? What happens when you tense up and find yourself just trying to hit the ball in the middle of the court? And to make things worse, what if your opponent takes advantage of your safe tactics and starts hitting winner after winner? If you find yourself in a situation such as this, try saying, "I played like the Ronald Reagan of tennis. Way too conservative."

90. I made too many mental errors.

As any top player knows, it's not enough to simply have good groundstrokes, a solid net game, and a powerful serve. To be really successful, you also need to be strong between the ears. The next time an unforeseen defeat comes a-calling, let all who will listen know, "Way too many mental mistakes today. Probably would have won if I had been thinking straight."

91. I've never double-faulted that many times before.

Playing poorly can surely be frustrating. Missing shots or moving slowly can really put a damper on your day. But in my humble opinion, nothing is as upsetting as double-faulting over and over again. I mean, when you can't even get the point adequately started, oh how upsetting! The next time you get a case of the yips, and find your service motion letting you down, try "The last time I had a service experience like this, I left a 5 percent tip."

Did You Know?

Did you know that Marc Rosset holds the record for the most double faults in a match when he threw in 26 doubles in a loss to Michael Joyce at Wimbledon in 1995?

92. My opponent is a big fat cheater!

This will work best when no one has been watching your match. Even if no one's there, stop and stare when there's the slightest question about your opponent's line calls. Then you can always explain a loss by telling your friends, "I wish you had been there to witness that guy's calls. He was hooking me the entire match!"

93. My opponent was in the zone.

I ask you . . . is there anything better than playing at your very best? Although they might not come often enough, those days when everything we touch turns to gold are simply the best. But what happens when your opponent is the one with the Midas touch? When your opponent is seeing the tennis ball like it's a beach ball, and he is on fire? Well, don't despair. Just let anyone who will listen know that "My opponent was flying so high he was in another atmosphere."

94. The court didn't play well.

This works best on clay, although you can also claim that a hard court is sinking in certain spots. While losing, complain that the ball isn't bouncing properly, and that there are dead spots on the court. And finally, "What's with the maintenance crew here? Someone's not doing their job. The ball kept dying when it came to my backhand."

95. I didn't want it badly enough.

This excuse is truly tried and true. In almost every major sporting event, you'll hear the losing team use it. You can be going at 110 percent, diving for balls, crashing into the fence, and end up bloodied and bruised. But if you end up in defeat despite your herculean efforts, no need to put your tail between your legs and bury your head. Just tell all who will listen that "I just didn't want it badly enough."

96. I've never played with this racket before, and I'm not used to it.

As any good therapist can attest, change is hard. And as most of us know, there will eventually come a time when it's time to make the life-altering decision to change rackets. As difficult as this is—it's like losing a dear friend—you can use this pain to your advantage by telling the victor, "I'm just not used to my new racket."

97. I keep taking my eye off the ball.

It's the very first rule in tennis. We learn it as soon as we step on to our first tennis court: "Keep your eye on the ball." It's an essential part of the game, and because every player knows it, that's what makes this excuse so a worthy one. If you tell your adversary that "For some reason I just couldn't keep my eye on the ball," it's sure to get you off the hook.

98. I was just too nervous.

Ever hear the expression "There is nothing to fear but fear itself?" That's all well and good, but when you're in a third-set tiebreaker trust me . . . the anxiety is palpable. But there's good news. You can use your anxiety to your advantage. No, not by harnessing the energy and playing better. But by using it as a more-than-valid excuse. The next time you lose a nail-biter, just say, "I was oh, so nervous. I thought I was going to pass out."

99. The sweet spot in my racket is just too small.

Is there a better feeling than hitting a perfectly placed winner with the sweet spot of your racket? That one moment of perfection can keep a player coming back time and time again just trying to repeat that moment of nirvana. But part of finding the sweet spot is having the right weapon in your hand. If you find yourself missing shot after shot, and to make matters worse your racket is vibrating like your cell phone, try this one on for size: "The sweet spot on my racket is just way too small."

Did You Know?

Did you know that in 1975, the American tennis brand Weed made the first oversize racket?

100. My sneakers are not appropriate for a clay court/hard court/grass court.

I used to know a guy who wasn't the best tennis player. His groundstrokes were weak, his serve was inconsistent, and his net game was nonexistent . . . but oh boy could he run. He used to always say, as he gets older and his opponents slow down, if he can just find some way to keep his wheels in check, he'll surely clean up. But a nice little ancillary benefit was that he always had a built-in excuse when he lost. Whenever the match didn't go his way, he would always rely on his old faithful, "I'm just not wearing the right shoes for this court." The next time you find yourself down and out, you might want to try slipping a bit, tripping over your own feet, or looking down at your shoes and cursing under your breath. Then, after the match, let everyone who will listen know that "If I had the appropriate footwear, this match would have turned out differently."

101. There was a speck of dirt on the ball, and it was driving me crazy.

In tennis, the ability to clear your mind and put all of your focus onto that little, yellow, fuzzy ball is paramount to being successful. That's probably why tennis requires its fans to be silent, and to sit still during the matches . . . any distraction can lead to failure. To use this excuse, you really want to throw on your "cleanliness is next to godliness" routine. Start by washing your hands before the match. Make sure your clothes are clean and pressed and your tennis bag is pristine. Then, if and when the unthinkable occurs, and you end up as a big, fat loser, just let your opponent know that "There was a little speck of dirt on the ball, and I just can't stand an unsanitary game. I'd like to stay and have a drink, but I really have to get home and clean my house."

102. The net was too high/low/loose/tight.

Tennis is a game of precision. Consequently, if your string tension is a little bit too tight or too loose, if your grip wrap doesn't feel quite right, or even if your headband is slightly askew, it can cause your game to go right into the proverbial toilet. And believe it or not, in professional matches, the net height is assessed often, just to make sure that it meets with the exact specifications. But we weekend hackers aren't afforded that benefit. I would bet a lot of my hard-earned money that the nets at my local public courts haven't been checked in years . . . oh, the inhumanity! So the next time you hit the tape, and the ball falls back on your side of the court, explain it by saying, "This crummy net height is clearly not up to regulations!"

103. My forehand/backhand/serve/overhead/ volleys abandoned me.

As we all know, tennis is a great game. And when everything is clicking, it can lead to the highest of highs. Unfortunately, it's not easy to play in the zone all that often . . . there are just so many things that can go wrong. Between your groundstrokes, serve, and net game, there are simply a multitude of things that can let you down. But the good news is we've all been there . . . so why not use it to your advantage? The next time one of the key components of your game goes awry, don't keep it to yourself. During the changeover, make sure to mumble loudly about how lousy your serve has been. Or in between points, you might even want to shout out to the tennis gods about how poor your net game has been. And when the match is over, and the inevitable defeat hits home, make sure tell your compatriots, "My (fill in the blank) has never been so bad!"

104. My opponent footfaulted.

For the 99.99999 percent of us tennis players who will never see the pro tour, it might not be a very glamorous game. Fun—yes. Exciting —sure thing. But glamorous, not so much. The locker room might not be too fancy. After a rainstorm, you will likely have to squeegee your own court, and the fanfare will likely be minimal to none. One of the many things we weekend warriors have to deal with is making our own line calls. But what happens if your opponent is footfaulting? It can be pretty difficult to make that call all the way from the other side of the court, yet it can give a player a distinct advantage, especially if they're a serve-and-volleyer. But luckily, there is something you can do to use this to aid your cause. And between you and me, maybe they only footfaulted once or twice. Of perhaps it was a questionable foot fault on a big point. Or maybe they were six inches behind the service line . . . I won't tell. So the next time you say, "That son of a gun must have footfaulted 15 or 20 times, and it cost me the match," it will be our secret.

105. I don't know how I lost . . . I was the best one at my camp.

Many youngsters revel in their camp experience. The carefree days. The summer air. No school to worry about. And my personal favorite part of camp . . . getting to play tennis every day. And if you excelled in your summer tennis pursuits, you may feel like you're unbeatable. So if the unthinkable occurs, and you go down in flames, try explaining the defeat with

"I don't know how this could have happened . . . I was the best player at my camp."

106. My opponent made bad line calls.

This excuse has been used for as long as the game has been played. We all know these players. The ones that live by the motto "When in doubt, call it out." Or the ever popular "If you're not cheating, you're not trying." I mean, is there anything as frustrating as hitting your shot two inches inside the line only to hear, "Ohhh, it just missed?" But at least you can now explain your misfortune with "That guy was hookin' me all day long, and it cost me the match!"

107. I lost track of the score.

We've all heard it before—the first point counts the same as the last. But as any tennis player will attest, some moments are clearly more important than others. Surely everyone will agree that if you double-fault at 40-love, you're not going to lose any sleep. But a double fault in a third set tiebreaker can spell disaster. So the next time you lose a nail-biter, let your opponent know, "I had no idea that was match point. If I had known, I would have amped it up a notch."

108. I haven't played since high school.

Of course you love tennis. And you play whenever you get the chance. But the good news is not everyone knows this. However, everyone will surely agree that no matter how good a player you are, if you are out of practice, you're clearly not going to play up to your best. So it will be our dirty little secret. The next time you get beat like a drum, explain it with "I haven't played since high school, and the only reason I lost is that I was out of practice."

109. I had a headache/stomachache/itching hemorrhoids/terrible constipation/a hangnail/gas. (Feel free to name an ailment of your liking.)

To feel well is to play well. Is there anything better than playing your best and feeling like a million bucks, to boot? Your old knees are solid, your bad back is loose, and you're ready to conquer the world. But alas, those days are gone. You're over the hill and spend most of your free time discussing your ailments with your old friends, who nod knowingly because they're going through the same things. Well, now there's good news. You can finally use your medical issues to your advantage. The next time you go down to defeat (especially if you lose to a much younger player), let them know that "My whole body hurts and I couldn't play to my potential . . . when you're my age, you'll understand."

110. I got used to the sun in my eyes, but then it got cloudy.

Playing tennis on a beautiful 75-degree summer day, with a mild cool breeze, under perfect conditions . . . Oh, it's just

paradise! But of course Mother Nature doesn't always coop-
erate. Changing weather patterns can cause you as much
trouble as your opponent's huge serve. But at least now you
can use it to your advantage. The next time you're getting
beat like you stole something, look to the weather gods for
help. And after your thumping, tell your opponent that you
surely would have given them a better match if "The stupid
weather wasn't making me so miserable."

111. My grip was too large/small.

Even if your grip is the right size, this excuse can save you
when you're in the midst of getting a good ol' fashion butt-
kickin'. At the point when the outcome of your match is a
foregone conclusion (in your opponent's favor, of course),
start to take some time between points while repeatedly
changing the position of your hand on the handle of your
racket. Between games, comment to your opponent that your
grip feels strange to you and ask him if it appears to be too
big. Then continue to fuss around with it and use body language to express your frustration. Switch to a different racket
and then throw up your hands because that grip feels too big,

as well. If you're using a wrap or an overgrip, take it off the handle and then complain that the grip now feels too small. By this time, your opponent might be distracted enough that you'll actually have a chance to win the match, but if you end up losing anyway, just make a show of angrily shoving your rackets in your tennis bag and launch into your most pitiful whine. Something like "You know what, I'm going to really give it to the club pro who recommended this grip! I felt great when we started the match, but how am I supposed to play decent tennis when he recommended the wrong grip size?"

112. It was too hot.

Excuse #16 cites one's battles with weather conditions. More specifically, if you're a bit stiff and sore, a toasty day can help you loosen up, but if it becomes clear that you're going to lose, here are a few tips that can bolster your excuse: First, complain to your opponent about the oppressive heat, then stall as long as possible between games. When he's about to serve, hold up your hand to indicate you're not ready. Wipe your brow frequently and snap the moisture from your fingers. Make a show of changing your wristbands

frequently, even if they're not wet. Take off your shoes and wring out your sweaty socks. Get inside your opponent's head by mentioning that he looks exhausted. Tell him he looks a little pale and ask if he's ever had to stop playing because he doesn't feel well. And finally, when he appears to have had enough of your antics, suggest that you call it a draw and go somewhere for a cold beer. By this time, he'll be so disgusted that he'll be happy to call it off. And after you've quaffed your first tall one, rub it in by saying something like, "Ahhh, that's better. It was just way too hot today. And by the way, you looked like you were about to collapse!"

113. I got sweat in my eyes.

The next time you're up against a superior player on a hot day, the first thing you need to do is to hide your headband. Make sure to let your opponent know that you can't believe how stupid you were to leave your sweatbands at home. And clearly, if your nemesis offers you one of theirs, politely decline, stating that it just wouldn't be sanitary. Then, throughout the match, make sure to rub your eyes often and squint like you've just been taken out of a year of solitary confinement. After the inevitable drumming is completed, and you go to the net for the customary handshake, if you really want to lay it on thick, you might even reach out and miss your opponent's hand, as you've clearly been blinded. And make sure to tell everyone in earshot, "The sweat in my eyes is nearly unbearable!"

114. The observers were rooting for my opponent.

It's hard enough to win under normal circumstances, but when your opponent has a cheering squad it's even worse. So how do you deal with it? Well, you can try ignoring them by forcing yourself to strictly concentrate and watch the ball like your life depended on it; or maybe get sarcastic and applaud right along with the audience, even when they're celebrating your unforced errors or double faults. Or how about this? Some people actually play at a higher level when the spectators are rooting against them, but if you're not that kind of player and your level of play goes down with every passing point (pun intended), you'll just have to face it: you're gonna lose. The challenge here is to not sound too pathetic or like sour grapes when you're explaining your loss. If you can do it without gagging, try the seminoble approach: "I gave it my all, but have to admit his supporters got to me and threw me off my game."

115. Allergies.

This is one that many of us can relate to. If you're one of the many among us who can't wait for the first nice spring day to wipe the cobwebs off of your racket and hit the courts, this excuse might do the trick. For with spring weather comes allergy season. With every missed shot, try throwing in a sneeze or two. After losing the first set and going down a break in the second, a little wheezing may be in order. And after the damage is complete, and the unfortunate loss has occurred, a coughing fit might just be the icing on the cake. When parting ways, you can wrap a nice bow on it by stating, "I love spring tennis, but these darn allergies are killing me . . ."

116. My opponent hit too many drop shots.

You're no wimp. Your play a big banger's game. Powerful ground strokes, serve and volley even on clay, second serve as fast as your first. Unfortunately, not all your shots stay in the court. In fact, you never quite know where the ball is going and you rack up way too many double faults. But that's not the point. You like the big game and have no tolerance for pushers and junk artists. So when you're up against someone who doesn't give you the pace you need and just keeps getting the ball back over the net while mixing it up with drop shots, it can be downright frustrating. The result? You'll inevitably overhit and produce error after error, while your opponent calmly keeps racking up game after game. Eventually you'll get so disgusted that you start calling him a "dinker," but he's unaffected by your taunts. Now the outcome is no longer in doubt, and you're about to suffer the embarrassment of losing to a guy who hits his forehand at about ten miles an hour. What to do? By no means allow the match to proceed to its conclusion. Fake an ankle injury and reluctantly forfeit, and when you talk about the match to your macho buddies, make a disgusted face and say, "Fuhgetaboutit. I could wipe that guy off the court if I wanted to, but why humiliate him? I'd rather go up against a guy who plays real tennis."

117. I got Har-Tru in my shoes.

This one can be kind of hard to pull off because at least some of that green stuff manages to sneak into everyone's sneakers. What you have to do is demonstrate that you have a ton of it in yours. So how can you go about it? The answer is sleight of hand. While the other guy's not looking, scoop up a generous handful of Har-Tru and put it your pocket. Then, when the match is over, sincerely congratulate him on his win. He knows you're a whiner, so it will throw him off if you actually compliment him for a change. Tell him how well he played, his strategy was brilliant, whatever. And here's where you have to be a little bit slick. While you're still talking, bend over to untie your shoes and distract him by calling his attention to something in another direction. That's when you have to deftly transfer the contents of your pocket into at least one shoe. Then, when he's looking at you again, dramatically spill the load onto the ground and act as if you're stunned. "Well, look at that! There's my problem! How did all that stuff get into my shoe?"

118. I got hungry.

Once again, you're getting your butt kicked, and you're looking for an excuse. Take some extra time between games and complain that you don't feel like you have any energy, then start to mope around on the court and ask your opponent if he has any hard candy or orange juice. This could backfire if you're playing an anal-retentive who has a stash of just about everything in his bag, but even if he offers you what you're asking for, just put on a hangdog look at the end of the match and croak out something like, "Phew, I am starving! My blood sugar must have tanked, and I just couldn't recover."

119. I didn't sleep well last night.

You'll need to set this one up by yawning conspicuously even before your match begins, thus establishing a can't-lose situation. If you win, you did so despite being half asleep. And if you lose, it happened because you were half asleep. It will also help if you sort of nod off while sitting between games, plus rubbing your eyes will help to sell your slimy charade. And when it's over, win or lose, pretend to be a good sport by offering congratulations (or condolences, whatever the case may be), especially if others are watching. Something like "Nice match. You played really well." (Just be sure to stifle another yawn while doing so.)

120. The dog ate my racket! Look! Here's the tooth marks!

Yes, you have my approval to sink this low. After all, if all's fair in love and war, what about tennis? But how to pull it off? Come on now, use your imagination. All you'll need is a sturdy kitchen knife or screwdriver, or maybe some kind of garden tool like a trowel with a sharp edge. Simply carve out a few nicks and paint chips on your frame. Just cosmetic stuff of course, not enough to actually affect the integrity of the racket, and apply your artistic talent to make it look authentic. Be subtle about it when your match begins. Keep your racket out of sight so your opponent won't notice anything. If you happen to win, put your racket away quickly so you'll be able to use this excuse when you lose in the future. But when you do lose (as usual), that's when you fake an air of frustration: "I knew I was going to lose today! Look at this! Can you believe I caught my dog chewing on my racket this morning? See these tooth marks? How could I concentrate when I was playing with damaged equipment?"

121. I want a do-over; a bug flew up my nose during match point.

This one could apply whether you're winning or losing, but let's depart from the theme of this book and assume you're actually about to chalk up a win for a change . . . It's 6-5 in a tiebreaker—match point—and you're serving, but true to form you choke and double-fault. Worse, you know yourself: once that lead elbow sets in, the match is as good as over. But wait. . . . Don't despair, there's still an option that will save you a modicum of self-respect. During your next service toss, stop suddenly, let the ball drop to the court, and paw at your nose while jerking your head around as if something has penetrated your nostril. Fake sneezing could also be a nice touch. Then insist on a do-over, explaining that a bug flew up your nose. Of course you're going to lose anyway, but forget about preserving any dignity. Scrunch up your nose and hang onto that excuse like grim death. And when the match is over, continue to complain: "Can you believe that? (sniff, snort)—I was just starting to get my second wind when that bug flew up my nose (more sniffing and snorting). And you know what? I think it's still in there!"

122. If I didn't have bad luck, I'd have no luck at all.

Some days you get the bear, and some days the bear gets you. But in your case, that darn bear is never on your side. The word "luck" isn't in your vocabulary. It just isn't fair. When your opponent's ball catches the top of the net, it climbs over to your side and drops in for a winner. But with you, it's vice-versa. Happens every time. It's uncanny!

Not only that, but the other guy's mishits invariably come off his racket with wicked spin, and you look like a clown while lunging at the ball and missing it completely.

And there's more:

- The sun shines directly in your eyes when you're serving but ducks behind a cloud when your opponent is on that side.
- Wind gusts flare up only on your service toss, never on his.
- Your fabulous topspin lobs get carried out by inches because the breeze changes direction just as the ball flies over his outstretched racket.
- When your opponent's at net, he's handcuffed by a forehand that you pound directly at him. But when he flinches away to protect himself—you guessed it—the ball bounces off the butt of his racket handle and caroms to the sideline for a winner.

So there's a reason you keep losing: It's not you . . . the tennis gods are against you.

Therefore, don't ever admit that you lost a match fair and square. Just put on your "poor me" face and call on Rodney Dangerfield's classic refrain:

"I tell ya, I don't get no respect. If it wasn't for bad luck, I wouldn't have no luck at all."

123. Those guys were talking to each other in Spanish! Are they allowed to do that?

You won't believe this! My doubles partner and I were trouncing these two Latino guys who spoke perfect English, but when we started to pull ahead, they switched to Spanish and then they started laughing a lot. I think they were making fun of us, but I wasn't sure so I didn't say anything, and the more they talked and laughed, the more we got distracted and began to make a lot of unforced errors. So what are the rules about that? Could we have protested that they were distracting us on purpose?

124. I felt sorry for the guy, so I threw the match just to make him feel good.

Okay—so now you've come to the point where you don't care how low you have to go. You're in a close match, and it looks like you might actually chalk up a win for a change. But when you're about to close it out on your serve at 40-love, match point, you get a case of lead elbow. You choke. You "apple up." You double-fault twice, then dump an easy volley into the net, and before you know it, your opponent grabs the win. What's worse, the next day a friend says he was surprised you lost to that opponent. Perfect time to put on the martyr act: "You know, just between us, I had three match points on my serve, but the poor guy looked so sad about losing, I just couldn't take it from him. So I blew the match on purpose, and you know what? It's a nice feeling to do a good deed once in a while." (Now here's the really challenging part. When your friend compliments you for being a classy guy, just nod your head humbly and do your best to keep a straight face.)

125. He had a natural advantage because he served lefty.

You have lost your match and now you're looking for an excuse, but you have a problem. The conditions were ideal for tennis. Temperature in the sixties, no humidity, calm air, cloud cover blocking the sun, court in perfect condition, courteous opponent, you have no physical ailments or equipment problems, and there were no distractions of any kind. And then you strike on an answer. The other guy was left-handed, and he had a big slice serve that went wide to your backhand on the ad court. You're not used to playing lefties. Otherwise you would have won easily. Of course your

Did You Know?

Did you know that although lefties only make up about 10 percent of the population, some of the best tennis players of all time were left-handed? For example, Rod Laver, Martina Navatilova, Rafael Nadal, Monica Seles, Jimmy Connors, and John McEnroe were all southpaws . . . just to name a few.

lefty opponent had a similar problem when receiving in the deuce court . . . your right-handed slice serves went wide to his backhand . . . but don't mention that. Chances are your friends will nod in agreement when you toss off a casual remark like, "You know how it is. Those lefty servers . . ."

126. Look at that guy's outfit. How can I concentrate when his shirt and his shorts clash?

If you're a club player, there's usually some type of dress code, like all whites or at least a shirt with a collar and shorts in a complementary color. But if you're a scrapper at a public court, it's often all bets off in the fashion department. Cut-off jeans and a ragged t-shirt are de rigueur, and you can't judge a book by its cover because there are plenty of 5.0 players who couldn't care less about what they're wearing. But sometimes a guy (or even a gal) will show up in a fashion statement that is just plain painful. Checkered orange-and-purple shorts with a polka-dot chartreuse top, or paisley and stripes. So if you aren't feeling at the top of your game, go out of your way to pick an opponent who's dressed like that, because if you lose, your excuse is built in: "Could you believe the way that guy was dressed? I could barely open my eyes to look at him, let alone watch the ball."

127. If I practiced as much as he does, I'd be just as good.

This guy drives you crazy. You're far more talented than he is, more athletic, better ground strokes, stronger serve, way more macho on the court. But he beats you regularly and he can't conceal a smug smile that makes you want to smash your racket over the net post. So how come he cleans your clock every time? Because he practices regularly, several times weekly, plus he's lessoned to death so even though he has no weapons and moves like a programmed robot, he keeps his eye on the ball and gets everything back. You have to play above yourself to chalk up a point, and this leads to a string of unforced errors that unnerves you and invariably ends up in a humiliating loss to a "pusher." But don't despair, you have a built-in excuse. Put on your best display of bravado and tell your friends, "Are you kiddin' me? That guy can't walk and chew gum at the same time, but he takes tons of lessons and hits against the ball machine for a couple of hours every day of the week. If I had the time and money to work with a pro and practice that much, I'd wipe the court with him."

Did You Know?

Did you know that former world number one Ivan Lendl was once quoted as saying, "If I don't practice the way I should, then I won't play the way that I know I can"?

128. He took a cell phone call between games, and it threw off my momentum.

This is an easy one. Explain your loss by complaining that your match was interrupted just when you were about to turn the tide. Your forehand was clicking, your volleys were crisp, and your serves were getting to be unreturnable. Then your opponent's phone rang and he took the call "and he kept me waiting for five minutes! . . . and without apologizing!

I was so furious that I couldn't concentrate. Otherwise, I would've trounced that guy!"

129. I got dehydrated.

In all athletic ventures, every trainer worth their salt will tell you that it's important to stay hydrated. Drink, drink, drink! And once you get thirsty, it's too late. This adage has never been more true than in the great game of tennis. And everyone knows it. The good news is you can use it to your advantage. On the next hot day, when the match is almost over, and it's more than clear that you're about to go down in defeat, feel free to use this excuse. When your opponent isn't looking, spill out your remaining water. Then, after the inevitable loss, hold your container upside down and let your opponent know that you've been out of the thirst-quenching liquid for the last set and a half. Last, you can end by saying something noble such as, "I'm parched . . . I just didn't want to interrupt the match to get more water."

130. I made too many mental errors.

One of the many reasons I love tennis is that it's not just a physical contest, but a mental game, as well. Sure, it helps to be strong, quick, and athletic, but without a strong mental game, your killer serve and groundstrokes will only take you so far. But somehow it's a more than acceptable excuse to blame your loss on mental mistakes. If you said, "I have a lousy serve" or "My backhand is terrible," that probably won't fly. But the next time you feel like the match is getting away from you, after each lost opportunity, make sure to point to your head and make a face that denotes disgust. You might even want to yell out to yourself to "Concentrate!" And after the carnage is complete, and you're shaking hands at the net, you might just try uttering, "I wish I could have given you a better game, but my mind just wasn't in it."

131. I ran five miles before my match, and I was too tired to play effectively.

This excuse works best if you're in decent shape and you look like it's plausible that you could have run five miles before the match. But if you've got a bit of acting skills, even if you're over the hill and carrying some extra weight, it just might work. First, you've got to lean against the fence between points. You might even want to feign a cramp and do some stretching. Finally, after the match is over, let your opponent know that "It was a major mistake to go on that long run before the match . . . I'm just exhausted!"

132. My masseuse is on vacation.

In order to play your best, you need to feel your best, as well. And clearly, a stiff and sore player is not going to be able to compete at their optimal performance. But a masseuse, you ask . . . really?! Well, all the pros have them. And if Roger Federer and Serena Williams use a masseuse, why can't you? So after your next loss, grab your back, roll your head in an attempt to stretch out your neck, and whine to anyone who will listen, "My masseuse went on vacation without letting me know. This is unacceptable! How can I be expected to play my best in this condition? I really need to find a more responsible employee."

133. I have terrible constipation.

This excuse can be a bit touchy. But desperate times call for desperate measures. If the match isn't going your way, make sure to continually grab at your stomach. You might even want to keel over in pain. And after the painful loss has concluded, make sure to put a sheepish expression on your face and let anyone who will listen know "It was hard to go after the ball, because it's just been so hard to go."

134. Those guys on the next court were spectacular.

So you've run out of plausible excuses and it's time to scrape the bottom of the barrel. Forget about integrity, or sportsmanship, or even basic human decency. You've got to come up with something, *anything*, no matter how pathetic or lame. So how about this after you've lost the last point and you meet your opponent at net, nodding your head in mock admiration: "Hey Man, I have to give you credit. I've seen you play better, but you seemed to be focused during the entire match. But me? I couldn't take my eyes off of those guys next to us. That lefty over there had a wicked backhand slice, and he was lethal when he came to the net. I don't know how you could concentrate. It seemed like every time I was about to start my backswing, one of them did something else even more spectacular." And then, with your most sincere expression, grasping his hand with both of yours for an earnest handshake: "Anyway, that's no excuse. It was your day, even though I think you'll agree that it was more a loss for me than a win for you. Maybe I can give you a better match next time so you can raise your game."

135. My socks kept falling down.

This is another one of these excuses that you have to prepare for in advance.

The first step is to choose a pair of long socks—like those geeky tube numbers that you buy in bulk, six pairs for $1.75. When your match begins, it will help if your opponent is the kind of guy who will rank on you about your knee-high hosiery, but in any case start playing with the socks all the way up. If you're winning, and the socks are annoying you for any reason, just fold them down so that they're wrapped around your ankle. But if you're losing, start to complain that they're bothering you, and be sure to make a show of tugging on them between points. Then, when you've gone down to defeat, your explanation is built in: "These crummy socks! I don't know why I even bought them. Next time I'll wear a pair that doesn't distract me while I'm playing." And then be sure to behave like a true sportsman by offering congratulations to your opponent (disingenuous, of course).

136. I have jock itch.

You'll have to be somewhat delicate with this one, especially if there are women or children nearby, but if it becomes clear that you're about to go down to ignominious defeat, just use your imagination: a scratch here, a tug there, scootching around uncomfortably while sitting between games . . . you get the idea. Then, if your opponent comments on your obvious discomfort, it will be simple for you to explain why you lost. But if he doesn't, how about something like "Have you ever had jock itch? Man, this is brutal. I couldn't concentrate on a single point."

137. I have hemorrhoids.

This is another condition that calls for a bit of discretion. Fortunately, there's a role model, none other than the magnificent Rafael Nadal. Not that the greatest clay court player in history has hemorrhoids, but I'm sure you've noticed his obsessive ritual before every point, one element of which is pulling on his shorts. What a perfect excuse: "I'm not trying to look like Rafa, but I've got a case of raging hemorrhoids that completely threw off my game."

138. I have a headache.

Probably the oldest excuse in the book, but who can argue with you when you complain that your head's killing you? Of course you'll have to lay it on thick, such as rubbing your temples and stretching your neck, or lying down with your eyes closed between points. The only problem is that your opponent might be carrying some aspirin or ibuprofen, and offer it to you. Still, you don't have to accept it. Use a polite refusal while holding your eyes shut with your thumb and forefinger. "Thanks, my head's throbbing, but I prefer to use meditation as a treatment rather than rely on Big Pharma." Now you not only have an excuse for losing, but you will also evoke sympathy for being a martyr.

139. I have a stomachache.

There's no doubt. You're going to lose. Solution? Easy. First, stop playing, ideally in the middle of a point, and rub your stomach. When your opponent asks if you're okay, just wave him off and pretend to soldier on despite your discomfort. Give it a point or two, then do the same thing, but this time bend over and pretend that you're about to throw up. Surely, even the most competitive opponent will offer to call off the match, but if you can keep a straight face, milk it a little longer. Finally, shake your head sadly and apologize with a parting remark like "Sorry, must have been something I ate. Too bad, because I thought we were having a great match."

140. The lines on the court were slick.

Who says tennis can't be a dangerous game? Just ask former tennis great James Blake, who literally broke his neck when he slipped and collided with the net post. From pulled muscles to throwing out your back, real tennis players know that there are true perils in this sport. And one of the most common injuries on the court occurs when a player takes a fall. Furthermore, if there is the slightest amount of moisture in the air, the lines on the court can become as slick as ice. So the next time you're playing poorly, and the court gets a bit damp, look down and slide your foot back and forth on the white stripes. Shake your head back and forth and mumble how dangerous the conditions are. Then, you can always explain your woeful effort with "The lines were slick and I was afraid I was going to go down like a sack of potatoes. How was I supposed to play well under these types of conditions?"

Bonus! Doubles Excuses

141. I was worried he was going to hit me in the head with his serve.

This guy's a maniac! He goes for broke on both his first and second serves, and he hits totally flat, so if his racket head is angled even a couple of degrees off center, the ball could go anywhere. He zipped one just past my ear, so I had to stand so far in the doubles alley when he was serving, the opponents had an open court for their return. So after your defeat, how about trying this one: "We could have won if I wasn't so worried about getting my head knocked off by an errant serve."

142. We both called "I got it" at the same time.

Our opponents lobbed a lot, and we both like to hit overheads. He's a lefty and I'm a righty, so we both take balls down the middle and I couldn't get the guy to stop taking my shots. Definitely not my fault! But don't despair, you can always explain your sorry performance with "Why can't I find a partner who listens to me?!"

143. I had a spat with my regular partner, so I had to call my amateur neighbor.

Talk about bad timing. My partner and I had words the morning of our match and he stomped off, so I had to scrounge up someone else. The only one available was my neighbor, who had asked me a hundred times to play. Unfortunately, he didn't have the first idea of how to play doubles. He was out of position most of the time, and even when he was able to return a shot, he would put it right on the opponent's racket. Just my luck. But fortunately, there is a built-in excuse. How about, "One of these days I'm gonna find a guy who knows how to play but isn't a head case!"

Did You Know?

Did you know that Pam Shriver is in the Hall of Fame despite never winning a singles Grand Slam tournament? However, Shriver is known as one of the most successful doubles players of all time. Shriver's longtime doubles partner was Martina Navratilova . . . unquestionably one of the greatest tennis players of all time.

144. We both prefer to play the forehand side.

Why does everything always happen to me? I was told this guy was a good doubles player, but it turns out that he's unwilling to compromise on who plays where. I could play in the ad court, but my forehand is a weapon and is much better than his, even though he disagrees. It seems like every one of my partners has an issue of some kind. . . . Hmmm, it couldn't be my fault, could it? Of course not. Just try this one on for size: "If my partner had only realized that I hit my forehand like a young Andre Agassi, the outcome would have surely been different."

145. My partner doesn't like to play the net.

As any good tennis strategist will tell you, to truly succeed in doubles you have to own the net. But my partner won't get off the baseline if his life depends on it. Who plays doubles like that? Once again, I drew a turkey for a partner. But even though the loss may sting, there is a silver lining. Just tell your friends, "If my partner was only willing to play traditional doubles and come to the net, we would have rushed them and crushed them."

146. My partner is a court hog.

Now here's a guy who manages to play singles on a doubles court. Even with balls that are well on my side of the court, I invariably hear, *"Mine!"* He'll cross over the center line by ten feet to take a ball that he has no business going for. Meanwhile, he misses most of them because he's out of position, and if he does manage to get it back, I have no time to cover his side, so the opponents just have to tap the ball into our open court. What's going on here? Is there no one out there who knows how to play this game? But alas, no need to fret. Just try this excuse: "If my opponent wasn't such a court hog, and learned to stay on his own side of the court, my superior game would have surely garnered us the victory."

147. My partner made me serve on the sunny side.

Is there no courtesy nowadays? I'm a lefty, so it's much more of a disadvantage for me to serve into the sun. This guy's right-handed, but he didn't want to hear it. Maybe he saw the error of his ways when I double-faulted a dozen times because I couldn't see the ball on my toss. We would have won easily if he wasn't so stubborn. Plus, now I think I have permanent eye damage. So after you get back from the eye doctor, try this excuse: "I normally have a killer serve, but you can't expect me to serve well when my toss goes directly into the sun."

148. My partner kept making bad calls, and it interrupted my concentration.

What was I supposed to do? If it happened once or twice, it wouldn't have been a big problem. But he was hookin' the other guys at least once a game, and when I insisted on reversing his calls, he went crazy and accused me of being a lousy partner. Once again, the tennis gods decided to have a good laugh at my expense. But not to worry. It will all work out in the end. Just tell 'em, "I guess I'm just too honest for my own good, and I can't stand to see this type of injustice."

149. My partner was so big, I couldn't serve around him.

I know, that sounds like a lame excuse, but man, the guy's a giant! Seriously, he could play, but I had to serve from the very edge of the court to get enough of an angle to put the ball in the service box. So the next time your serve gets broken like a bad promise, you can always explain your serving woes with "It wasn't my fault that I couldn't hold serve. I really think we would have won if I had served from my usual spot."

150. My partner wore black socks, and the fashion faux pas distracted me.

Seriously. Who wears black socks? Every time the ball came to me, I saw those goofy things out of the corner of my eye. So after a loss, try this one on for size: "Somehow our opponents weren't bothered, but I'm sure the reason we lost was because my partner looked like a fashion 911."

151. My partner had a weak serve.

Tough day today. I was booming my serve, and on half of them the return was so weak that my partner at net had easy sitters that anyone could put away. So I held serve every time, but did he hold up his end? No way! In fact, his serves were so weak, I had to move back to the service line so I wouldn't get killed on the return. Needless to say, we lost in straight sets. And then he had the nerve to say, "Well, we gave that one away." "*We?*" Now I ask you, do I not deserve the Nobel Peace Prize for resisting the urge to break my racket over his head? Trust me, I'm going to tell everyone who will listen that "If my partner's serve had been any weaker, I could have ended up in the hospital."

152. I was distracted because my opponents kept high-fiving each other.

Can you believe those guys? It's one thing to celebrate when you win a tough rally, but every time they won a point they acted like they just won the US Open, even when I gave them a gift by double-faulting or making a pathetic unforced error. Come on. Show a little class. Act like you've been there before. So how could I concentrate? You can explain this one by stating, "The only reason we lost is because I couldn't stand their shenanigans. What a couple of clowns!"

153. My partner kept blaming me for every point we lost.

Please. Like it was never his fault. Even when he blew a shot, he'd complain that I was out of position, or it was my shot in the first place. In fact, he was the one at fault most of the time. So when am I ever going to find a doubles partner who can actually play tennis and also has some idea of sportsmanship and social skills? It's just one bozo after another. Surely it's not my fault, don't you agree? Come on! I'd be the top doubles player in my league if I had a decent partner! If you find yourself in this type of situation, a more than valid excuse is "My partner really needs to take the responsibility for what was obviously his failure . . . not mine."

154. My opponents wore identical yellow outfits, and it was too hard to concentrate

In all sports, the ability to focus is generally a key component to success. But the ability to concentrate in tennis is of such utter importance that the crowd is supposed to remain silent during the points. Can you imagine 20,000 screaming fans at the US Open while the players were trying to serve, or play a big point? It just wouldn't happen. But sometimes it's not just the noise that can be distracting. Sure, I get it, sometimes doubles teams will wear identical outfits. However, if they take it too far, and the clothes become distracting, it can make for a perfect built-in excuse. So how about "Our opponents' outfits were so distracting that I couldn't concentrate on a single shot."

155. My partner was not wearing tennis sneakers, and it was tearing up the court.

This excuse works best if you're playing on a clay or grass court where the surface is more vulnerable. If you notice that your partner isn't wearing the proper foot attire, you can surely blame every bad bounce on the chewed-up court. So the next time you mishit a ball, or bury a ball into the bottom of the net, feel free to try this one on for size: "My partner's illegal footwear scuffed up the court and made it nearly impossible to play."

156. My partner kept hitting his returns right at the net player.

As any astute player knows, the key to doubles is taking over the net. So what's the remedy? Obviously to avoid the net player at all costs. Hit crosscourt whenever possible. Keep it away from the player at the net. But what happens when your partner is always trying to be the hero by trying to pass the net player with a winner in the alley? And to make matters worse, the net player continually stays home and picks off each attempted passing shot for a volley winner. Just explain the loss with "If my partner had kept it away from the player at the net, we could have definitely won that match."

157. My partner made too many errors.

As any experienced player can tell you, the most important decision you can make in doubles is to pick a good partner. However, if your partner ends up being a bust (or even if they don't—I won't tell), this is a great built-in excuse. Just like it takes two to tango, it takes a joint effort to put forth a win. And if you end up with a big, fat loss, you can always say, "If my partner hadn't been so error-prone, we surely would have won."

158. My partner kept telling me where to play on the court, and it got really annoying.

In doubles, like any team sport, communication is of paramount importance. But I ask you, dear reader, is there anything more annoying than when your doubles partner is continually telling you where to play on the court? "You're in no-man's-land." "Rush the net." "Stay back." And to make it worse, the partner who seems to give the most advice always gives the worst advice. So the next time your team is down a set and a break, and the outcome looks bleak, pretend to cover your ears when your partner spits out their two cents. Feign a look of utter annoyance. Then, after the match, make sure to tell your compadres that surely you could have won the match if only your partner hadn't been so "gosh darn annoying."

159. My partner kept lobbing, but both of our opponents were 6-foot-4.

As any good tennis player knows, a lob can be an effective shot on the tennis court—especially in doubles, when your opponents are crowding the net. But when it seems as if you're playing against a couple of Amazons who have booming overheads, this technique just might backfire. And when the powerful smash winners start to add up, make sure to sigh loudly. You might even want to mumble under your breath, "Not another lob." Then, after the handshake at the net with your inevitable defeat, you can let your opponents know, "Great match; next time we might even be able to give you a real challenge if I can get my partner to stop lobbing so much."

160. My back hurt from carrying my doubles partner.

In today's modern game of tennis, you may have noticed that the top players require an entourage. The world's best players have a personal coach, a stringer, and even an accountant to help manage their millions. But perhaps the most important enhancement to winning would be a good chiropractor. Just ask anyone who has ever lost a match and said, "Oh, my achin' back!!"

161. I thought it was yours.

This excuse is truly a classic. It's been used by top professionals and husbands and wives since doubles was invented. Your team is in the optimal position. You're hunkered down at the net and are ready to knock off a volley to take command of the match. It's at that very moment where your opponent hits a ball right up the middle, dividing you and your opponent like Moses did with the Red Sea. The match quickly turns from your advantage to a likely defeat. That's when you clear your throat and in your loudest voice let anyone in earshot hear you say, "I thought it was yours!"

162. My mixed-doubles partner's cute behind distracted me.

This excuse is especially good for those of you with an overactive libido. You're paired up to play mixed doubles with a really cute partner. You're doing your best to impress, but you can't keep your eyes off his/her derriere. You're trying to concentrate, but every time your partner reaches down for a low ball, you almost pass out from passion. It might cost you a slap in the face, but you can try telling your partner, "Sorry, but your skirt is so short I couldn't help looking at your behind the entire match."

163. My doubles partner was constantly trying to teach me while we were playing.

As a licensed psychologist, I have learned one piece of very important information over the years. Never, EVER give advice unless someone is asking for it. Well, the same can be said in tennis. Sure, you might be willing to pay good money to get the local pro to give you some helpful tips. But what you don't want is for your doubles partner to pepper you with suggestions during a friendly game. And don't even get me started if you partner is a relative, e.g., a spouse, sibling, or parent. Oy . . . it can just be soooo annoying. The next time your partner is trying to constantly tell you how to improve your backhand, or hit a better serve, midmatch, tell your friends, "Can you believe that guy was trying to teach me how to play?! It was just so distracting!"

164. No wonder they won. They played one up and one back. How can you play good doubles like that?

You like to play tennis the right way, especially in doubles, where the strategy is obvious: get to the net! And when they lob, smash your overhead so hard they're quaking in their sneakers. No way you can lose that way. But big surprise: they beat you with one guy on the bascline ... and sometimes both of them were back there! No biggie: simply tell your friends, "Can you believe it? They played the match with at least one of them on the baseline! Personally, I'm not a fan of this wimpy version. The only reason we lost is I was too disgusted to play that way."

Epilogue

So remember, my fellow tennis lover, always play your hardest. Always work for every point. Always do your best. But at the end of the day, if the unthinkable has occurred, and you have lost the most important point of the match (the last point), you'll have nothing to fear. Now you'll be able to explain to anyone who will listen why you're so inferior, why you're such a poor player, why you're such a loser. You can explain it all with *It's Not My Fault: 150 Excuses Every Tennis Player Should Know!*